MOREMY PRESENTS...

The Celibacy Chronicles

BY: MORGAN RENAE MYERS

Copyright © 2017 by Morgan Renae Myers

All Rights Reserved. No parts of this book may be reproduced in any form without the express written consent of Publisher/Authors, except in the case of brief quotations embodied within relevant articles and book reviews for print ad electronic media.

Acknowledgments

I would first like to give honor and thanks to the Creator and my ancestors that watch over me, guide me, protect me and love me on my journey as a spiritual being having a human experience here on Earth. Those that came before me that make what I do possible. I feel their energy and presence with me in real-time. Next, I give honor to my parents, Alfreda Myers and Timothy Silver who were the vessels through which my life was birthed; without their mutual connection, there would be no me. I want to thank my family, for just being who they are. Our connectedness or lack thereof teaches and motivates me to be true to myself; they've helped me recognize the true definition of what family is and is not; how our differences make us the beautiful, conflicted, dramatic, intelligent, resourceful, and kindred roots of one another.

I commend and applaud every teacher I've ever had in my lifetime, in and outside of the classroom. You all challenged me to think outside the box, you also required more of me and even when I was too talkative to listen, the lessons always came back and showed themselves.

I cannot acknowledge my community enough; North Carolina in general, Greensboro specifically, with a focus on those in alignment with sharing the arts, economic and community empowerment. My community friends which have become family truly uplift and motivate me. I want to thank three of my closest friends Sister Monyia, Brotha Kain and Brotha T. Walker whose conversations sparked a fire up under me to compile this book in such a short amount of time. Their personal success, coupled with their belief in me to "use what I got"' held me accountable for not wallowing in self-pity, but utilizing my voice to find the freedom of expression I've been seeking. I'm extremely grateful to my friends Brittany Bellanger and Jeron Walston opening the doors of their home to me at a time I needed housing the most. While living with them I've been able to sit, think and take action over my life, in a comfortable home, have not starved and have been able to create freely, thus this book got started and completed under their roof. (Thanks for letting me use your computer when mine suddenly stopped working Britt). I quit my part time job and moved out of my apartment in May 2017 to go on a spiritual journey, just to have my car break down a week into the journey. I ended up back in NC and added value to two different friends' homes who so graciously allowed me to lay my head and get my life together (thank you Clarity and Sheena). I believe I got too comfortable and life had to teach me a lesson in procrastination and finally following my passion. I haven't been homeless, but I've been without a home of my own for half a year. These community minded friends' selflessness is appreciated and never forgotten.

A tremendous shout out to all the collaborative artists that agreed to be a part of this book and self-love movement. All but one artist lives in NC (made that ATL to NC connect). Some I already knew others I met online and a few in the community live painting at poetry shows. The excitement they all displayed to be a part is humbling. Their words of gratitude for being included as a way to gain extra exposure, commissions and conversation around their pieces brings me the most joy. Bringing artists and economics together is one of my passions. For your time, effort, creativity, open mindedness and leap of faith in collaborating with me, Dare Coulter, Tyamica Mabry, Ahanayzha Mabry, Ebonique Day, Daylon Owens, Sydney Nicole Abbott, Kaleye, Nycci James, Dwayne Howell aka Dr. How, Kendra Washington, Sherrita C. Williams, Sean Mulkey, Erran Hamlin, Kindra Thomas aka Soul Sistah Kae (waist beads/ chastity belts) and Brandon Brockington aka Mr. B Rock (poetry pins), I give thanks for your being as you help my dreams manifest with your presence alone.

I would be remised not to mention the guidance from the editors who helped make this book a tangible object. Sister Monyia and Brother Kwame of Copper Vibrations have always shown their support for me from our initial meeting. Encouraging my poetry and crochet business, we have bartered to the ends of the earths to work with one another. Having been authors prior to their jewelry business, their willingness to help and guide me through this process has been a breath of fresh air. To my poetry coach and mentor, Rakeem Person who tells it like it is; the truths I need to hear about my writing (I haven't found anyone else that has the courage to), I give immense thanks. You have worked with me on my writing and performance since college and I know I can attribute much of my writing growth to your guidance to help me Find My Voice.

The bulk of this project I am graciously indebted to the investors whose financial push made this possible. Sister Makeda Gordon who has become a life mentor (whom I met via Facebook) teaching me the principles of being an Empress. Her book "Lord Why Am I Not Married: Because You're Not Single" taught me a lot about myself and was an inspiration to continue being honest about my journey. To my Alpha brother Jordan Jones; thank you for being so dope, supportive and believing in me. To all my Sorors of the Illustrious Omega Nu Chapter of Zeta Phi Beta Sorority Inc. Ya'll have showed up and showed out for me, like only a loving sister LIKE YOU could. This project was able to happen due to your contribution and I give eternal thanks for it. Soror(s) Jacqueline Pippens, Audrey T. Hogan, Milagros Rivera Russell, Jennifer Jones, Brenda Livingston, and Lisa Ferguson.

Finally, I would love to thank all of you, the readers, supporters, community members, family and friends that have purchased a copy, poured a kind word into my life, followed my Facebook posts, left feedbacks, or ideas. If this is your first time connecting with me, I hope it won't be your last. I pray you get something out of my experiences and lessons learned, expressed in this poetically honest project. If I may make a request, no matter what, love yourself the best.

Peace, Love, & Light,

Morgan Renae Myers

2017

Foreword

There are poets who cloak their secrets in metaphors and rhythmic nuances that cause subconscious fingers to snap—yet the owners of those fingers miss something important: the truth. Morgan Myers writes with such honesty, such transparency, that readers will not miss the importance of her truth. The collection that you are about to enjoy is one that is composed of more than just words, more than just rhyme schemes, more than just metaphors.

This collection is composed of the atoms of experience and self-reflection.

Morgan Myers is a poet who courageously bares all in her work. She does so lovingly. She does so assertively. She does so communally. Anyone who has witnessed this poet speak on any stage will now witness the same vulnerability and fearlessness in her written work. Anyone who has conversed with this poet will hear, in their own minds, a poet's truth resonating within them.

Morgan's genuine spirit and desire to enlighten others on the pitfalls of loving ideals and other people more than loving oneself will leave its mark. It will be a mark readers should wear proudly. To be marked by this poet is to be invited into your own experiences with the guidance of one who has discovered revelation in relations.

The Celibacy Chronicles is the cold shower this society needs. Don't be afraid to get wet. Step in. Be naked. Discover yourself.

Rakeem OneVoice Person
Poet, Editor, & Performer

TABLE OF CONTENTS

TIPSY...1

SELF-LOVE...4

SANGRIA SORROWS...8

INCOMPATIBILITY...13

SCARED PREGNANT...16

THE GET UP & GO...17

THE BLACK HOLE...22

PURITY...25

WOMEN'S EMPOWERMENT...27

VAGINA O.O.O. (OUT OF ORDER)...31

SACRED...36

SPIRITS...40

WOMB RAGE...42

LUST DEMONS...46

WAKE UP CALL...49

INFLUENCED...52

CONVERSATION WITH GOD...55

Artist: Sean Mulkey

Moremy Presents.... The Celibacy Chronicles

Nip Slips
French kiss
Words drip
With lusty leaks
Stimulated by the eardrums
and heartbeats
Two dogs in heat
One an alpha male, the other a bitch
because he's already claimed a lady
But he's engaged in this moment
Licking his lips at you.
You feed into his bowl of mixed emotions.
His words and thoughts provoking
You promised to simmer down
But right now
He's stroking your ego.
Reminding you what your luscious lips are known for
"Don't be a whore"
You tell yourself.
As you mentally undress.
You remember the party punch
The reason he and you are even acting this way
You're influenced.

Moremy Presents.... *The Celibacy Chronicles*

Throughout the years

You and him wouldn't normally do this.

Bodily fluids

Begging to be released

You know you have the means to please

But you can't get the picture of her smile

and her ring

Out your head

So, you charge this moment to both of his heads

and not his heart.

Sometimes you just want to be your true self

Minus the Spirit, but keep the flesh

Through the daily agendas and commitments

You just want to relax in the comfort of friendship

and having the festivities end with a night cap

Doesn't sound so bad.

But instead you text and you laugh

and you word play, and you sober up and you drive away

Without anything to say the next day...

Moremy Presents.... *The Celibacy Chronicles*

Artist: Daylon Owens

Moremy Presents.... *The Celibacy Chronicles*

Self-Love

Self-love sometimes looks like:

crying in bathtubs

as you scroll down your timeline

and see nothing but inspirational

quotes and Black Love.

Staring in mirrors and giving yourself a hug.

Looking, listening, listing all of your flaws

then smiling, because you can either improve

or sulk about them.

Self-love looks like not being nervous every month

if you're pregnant; because you're celibate

and you can clearly count

how many cycles you had

since you last went to bed.

Self-love looks like not associating with drama

on TV, in real life, in your home.

You value yourself enough to

not just hold on to hurt

out of comfort—you'd rather be alone

Self-love looks like writing this poem.

After having shied away from writing and releasing

It's a healing medium
Feels like freedom
Self-love looks like turning off electronics
and tuning in; deep breathing.
Believing.

Self-love sometimes looks selfish...
because you choose to stay in the house reflecting
instead of in the club dancing
or on your phone responding to reckless text messages.
Self-love looks like taking care of your health;
mental, spiritual, physical, emotional
It looks like accepting constructive criticism
and not taking offense.

Self-love looks like when I see you, I see me.
Somehow, we're connected intricately
Out of all the places to be on the planet
it's in your presence I'm standing
so this moment has to be a part of my plan
of personal growth and expansion.

Self-love sounds like music.
Groovin'...highways to new places with many stops

Along the way.
It's sceneries never seen but felt immediately.
Its therapy...sharing...daring yourself
to get over yourself so you can be
your true self and reflect that Inner G;
That God within you that is also within me
Sometimes self-love sounds like silence.
Quieting our minds.
Putting the past behind us.
Learning from lessons, counting your blessings
and through all the trials
not stressing.
It's getting in the flow,
reading a good book,
feeling inspired,
transforming your mind.
Self-love is a requirement before dating and marriage.
It becomes apparent some internal work is needed to
propel.
Self-love sometimes looks like working for yourself.
Self-love is honest and true.
How can you love everyone else,
and forget about the most important person
YOU.

Moremy Presents.... *The Celibacy Chronicles*

Artist: Tyamica Mabry

Sangria Sorrows

Sipping fermented grape juice

to ease the pain

to stop the mind

from focusing

on things unwanted.

Soothing to a soul so free

it easily gets taken advantage of,

especially after one too many cups.

Yet it's harder being sober sometimes,

dealing with realities and lies

hidden behind the eyes of truths

standing in front of you

Why ...do we bring drama to our "loved ones"?

Here's a toast to the real ones

who have fussed me out, got great sleep

and still was able to talk with me about me

Learned where we both needed to grow

and mutually decided whether communication should cease

Let's pour this down the drain

for all those stolen moments and memories

When you didn't know how to say the things you needed to

You found your words now and I don't know how

but I just don't feel the same way

about me +you then as I do now.

Values and drinking don't correlate

I've just been thinking

I don't know if moving forward can replace

the grapes that have already soured

and won't make this next batch.

The taste too off-putting for Sangria connoisseurs

I've been here before:

oceans of tears and wanting you near

but now I realize you're fighting your little boy.

And we're using each other as an escape

That's why we can relate

but these grapes are sooooooo sour now.

Think it's time we put the glasses down,

pretend we're past it and go separate ways

Dirty wine stains

The party has ended

It's after 2 a.m.

and this bottle is empty.

Moremy Presents.... *The Celibacy Chronicles*

Photographer: LyricallUniqSoul

Moremy Presents.... *The Celibacy Chronicles*

Moremy Presents.... *The Celibacy Chronicles*

Artist: Ebonique Day aka Lady Picasso

Incompatibility

Love

You wouldn't do the same

So why would I catch a grenade

For some emotion that I live on in vain?

Veins as signs of memory

I'm not free from myself

I attempted to give you my all

But you left

From the very beginning I thought I loved you

Blinded by the mirage, of it, obviously

Wishing wells were meant for bedazzled princesses

To hope and dream at their broken complexes

well I'm wished upon by this feeling of Incompatibility

Cause for some reason I'm not that captivating really

This feeling wishes to destroy me and tear me down

Blindfold me, cover my ears and mouth

So that I can make no sound

Incompatibility wishes upon me the feeling of resent

So that every time I recall a historic emotion I repent

It leaves me wandering with no source of connection in sight

No one to reboot my battery when the charge gets low

No one to hold my hand when the tides get slow
No one to stand between me and God
No one to appreciate my thickness, which can be toned up in different places
No one who places me on any type of pedestal
No one who looks at me for my character and not my assets
Because ass and titties is always best...

I just want what every other girl wants
To be loved
And yes, I know it's too much to ask
And that's why I don't hold back
I see love and I cannot exist simultaneously
Not in a world, where I can't make up my mind what's right for me
When I choose to be the center of abuse
And then attempt to stop cold turkey
One minute I'm sexing some girl's man
Forced to be a part of the 20%, while she's still a part of the 80%
Yet I intend to become some one's 100.

The next minute I'm in wait of a blessing
Not so much looking
But hoping very much
That just for once the tables will turn

In favor of me

From a love in misery to one of

Compatibility

Moremy Presents.... *The Celibacy Chronicles*

Scared Pregnant

And out of
my womb
flowed you
    My seed
      I'd been so terrified
        that you
          survived
          fertilized
          a
            living
              breathing
              Self, growing
                inside
            Pushing aside hips
              stretching my outsides
                  nipples tender
              I remember praying,
                no, *pleading*
          no milk would start leaking
                  Was bloated
            scarred psychologically
felt like my stomach was housing a ball for bowling
            All my shirts felt too tight
        I looked locked and loaded
          that glorious day came
      late or on time I don't know
    13th day of the month I thank you
        You tortured me no more
  Relief at this release left me overjoyed
      No babies on this board
        At least not yet,
Done scared myself pregnant

The Get Up & Go

You know the feeling

When you're never being asked out?

But you're always being asked to lay down

On your back, at their house

Behind their girlfriends back?

Well if you don't know

It's not a good feeling

Momentarily, yes, I'm willing

But when something's in constant rotation

There's a time when it must end

And this spree of giving up my self-respect

To men who only want to make a fantasy out of me

Is now over...

Like that time

I was coaxed into unprotected, sexual intercourse

Yet again

This one was no friend

Moremy Presents.... *The Celibacy Chronicles*

No connection, communication, background information

Just a cute, dread head, thugged out nigga at a house party

He was dj-ing, I was all up in his space

He was rubbing and caressing by end of the night all up in my face

Underneath the covers on a ripped blue couch

I asked that he use protection

But he never did

Erection pushing through tight closed walls that were ready but not so willing

The warmth of his girth in me

Didn't subside the fear of what I was participating in

Unprotected sex with a man whose last name I was unfamiliar with

Sexual past I had no recollection of

He told me not to worry he wasn't gonna come in me

But I couldn't help but think, what type of brotha is this

Is he intentionally giving me HIV?

Or something worse?

The part that hurt is when he did cum

Inside of me

Made my heart bleed

First time that's ever happened

I was shocked, and he just placed his penis back in his pants and dipped

Flipped the covers over me as if the trash had been discarded

No more use of this easy target

I scrambled to wipe my vagina quickly

Before the semen began to seep

I know once sperm hits the surface the cells die

But what about the ones inside me that were released?

He didn't even quickly come out

He came and laid and waited in ecstasy

The morning after

A stranger coming so freely in me

I rushed to CVS to purchase Plan B

God, I hope this works for me...

I'm too close to kids and STD's

I'm through with the Get Up and Go

Come over, laugh, joke, and remove clothes

Make it as quick and unsensual as possible

Get dressed and leave

It's no longer my thing

I now become disgusted with the thought

I can't have passionate encounters

With people that enjoy my company

I'm not blaming these men for my actions

I understand if I'm handing out jewels for the taking

Why not rock them?

But it's time I lock them

Put back in a box for keep sake

Learn to WAIT

Looking for acceptance through every man

That pays miniature attention to me

Are these few minutes of thrusts

Gonna override my crying eyes at night?

No

It's time for old habits to die.

You're dismissed

Get Up & Go

Moremy Presents.... *The Celibacy Chronicles*

Artist: Kaleye

Moremy Presents.... *The Celibacy Chronicles*

The Black Hole

Emotionally inconsistent

A heart readily available to love

Locked out for fear of past feelings, once present

Now, become so unnecessary.

But comfort holds me back along with complacency

Here lately

It's been harder getting use to

Loving me

So that I may receive the one of my dreams

Nightmares exist because I live in them

The star of my own freak show

Being the pawn of seduction for men

Tricking my flesh into thinking this is all I'll ever want

The fun, freedom and fulfillment to mess with

Tom, Dick and Harry's hairy genitalia

I know... I'm more than my areoles, labia and cervix

But for me it doesn't seem that way

When I'm forced to face free time

In a home alone

Where thoughts are allowed to run wild

My body yearns for company

But it pains her to confront being lonely

So she finds guys to provide temporary stimuli

To the only place love can be disguised

Trembling cause my hands tied

Not to a bedpost

But to a concept affecting my health

Disturbing my mind and personal growth

I loathe what brought me here

I must fight 'til I get out

I bind the spirit of un-forgiveness and declare generational curses broken

I don't have to define myself or find my love by keeping my legs open

These broken in bedsprings

Lean not unto their own understanding

That the girl's body above is being branded

On another notch of the belt of insecurities and mistakes

It takes a messed-up person to get turned on from self-hate

Here lately, love can't be found in my loins

So I'll revert back to poems

Wrap up my insecurities, reposition my knees for prayer

Gag on gospels I share to keep young girls away from there

That place of lonely

Where black holes become their universe

Preventing light and life to shine through

We ladies are the galaxy of God

Enumerated stars

Ever present, ever shining

So to know, love and understand your solar system

Is more important than being blinded by every mushy, milky man that looks your way

Believe me it took gravity, STD's and God's mercy to pull me back to reality

Finally I realized it's my time to shine

Embrace my alone & quiet times

I invited peace and prosperity over to keep me company and stimulate me in ways unfelt before

Time's up for closing doors and throwing away keys

I'll start by loving more of me

Before turning to external factors to be pleased.

Moremy Presents.... *The Celibacy Chronicles*

Purity

Innocence
Virginity
Abstinent
Premarital
Violation
Celibate
Loose
Free Spirit
Cautious
Emotional
Sporadic
Balance
Neglected
Nuisance
Deprived
Dysfunction
Disease
Single
Self-restraint
Solitude
Sacred
Scared
Powerful
Treasure
Jewel

Moremy Presents.... *The Celibacy Chronicles*

Artist: Kendra Washington

Women's Empowerment

I'm a fun person, I enjoy a good time

Yet there are certain events that occur

Where I am reminded

I am phenomenally woman

Phenomenally me

And some men's reaction to this

Is somewhat off key

You see, they fixate feelings based on a desire they wish to pursue

But I'll give you men an example of what you won't do:

Ah ma!!! Yo shorty!! Dannnngggg Girl! Ah Yo Sexy mama!! (Come ere, Let me talk to you)

First of all your approach is incorrect, so I shouldn't even be addressing you

But since you're interested, I'll give you a taste of what to look forward too

Ma? Shorty? Girl?

I am woman.

Beautiful, black, woman.

I have yet to birth any children, thus have not earned the title of a mother or (ma) as you put it

With or without these heels, I tend to stand over you not only in stature but in mindset as well

And girls typically lean solely on the parental influences in their life, and I am very much so responsible and holding my own

I am the "Balance" of sweet black essence that Nikki Giovanni speaks of

I hold my head up high for the black girl hung down in Dixie that Langston speaks of

I know for myself that I am black, and I am woman

I am educated, strong and determined

I am evolution of empowerment, I am courage

I am loud, opinionated and a voice for my young sistas

My breasts sit high as proof that this long life ahead of me is not yet over

My hips are wide to block the discouragement that shall approach from all angles

My legs are long, and my arms are strong to climb mountains and reach goals

My eyes are brighter than my future

And my mind has no limits

So when approached by a man, I expect these things to be apparent

But since, young sir, you didn't recognize it, I decided to share it

A Phenomenal woman Maya Angelou once told me that: "people will forget what you said, people will forget what you did, but people will never forget how you made them feel."

So I ask you...come again?

If the man has even stayed through that empowerment speech on how not to approach me

He might then reply

"Alright, you're absolutely right!" Sorry I bothered you. Uh...I gotta go...

Moremy Presents.... *The Celibacy Chronicles*

Artist: Dr. How

Moremy Presents.... *The Celibacy Chronicles*

Vagina O. O. O (Out of Order)

I'm having complications with my vagina right now

She is currently out of business

Shut down
Out of order

Out of town

Catch her when you can

You can't

Because the extra storage she been paying in rent

Is all spent

All occupants

Have been evicted

This time it's serious

All of this...

Hasn't been worth just being curious

It's all fun and games in the beginning

Until something mama says

Comes back into the forefront of your memory

Leave something to be desired child

I think I took it too literal

I made my poonani the only thing about me desiring

And therefore was a pick 4 like the lottery

Countless numbers of bodies in and outside of me

I probably could call this a hobby

But now I'm acknowledging the problems with being too free

Sometimes you'll get chlamydia

Other times HPV

Sometimes you can take a pill to cure your STD

Sometimes you just D.I.E.

My complications equal hesitation

To just let any old phallus

Back inside these birth canals

A girl gone wild, ready to simmer down

Is less appealing for the taking now

Prior suitors not used to waiting around

New ones dismiss themselves once they realize it's shut down

It's my black holes, self-love, and wake up calls that keep me accountable now

Yoni steams, good reads and exercise that relieve my stress

I want a real love but been settling for less

Abusing my blessing

My portal to creation is sacred and worth the wait

Consistent quick anybody's, over one soul mate?

Vagina power!

In possession by the ladies

We set the standard for who and what comes out of these things

If we required more from ourselves and our partners

Meaningless sex wouldn't be an option

We'd all be penetrating to prosper

And men, your penis has importance too

So it don't need to be up in everything appealing you see move

You see without me, there's no you

And vice versa

So we're equally responsible for respecting the vagina

It's time to use our minds

Take pride in our value and who we share that with

Not everyone spirit need to be swapped

Energy is real

And transferable

Intimacy can be reached without the spreading of cheeks

Moremy Presents.... *The Celibacy Chronicles*

I get more turned on when they tap that intellect

Put our decisions in retrospect

Make me wet at just the thought of their dialect

I'm shut down now because I have self-respect

Covering my cookies

Cow milk is for calves

So before I dip this pretty brown almond back on any old mound

I'll know it's worth the exchange

Our connections will raise vibrations

Stimulations that elevate nations

My self is sacred, and my stuff is good

And I've found love, patience and value in myself,

Just like I should

Moremy Presents.... *The Celibacy Chronicles*

Artist: Erran Hamlin

Sacred

My self is sacred
And my stuff is gooooood
That's why I can't give it
to just any and everyone
For a while
I was misunderstood
I figured
I'm grown
I'll do whatever with whomever
Whenever I think I should
Luckily I never got pregnant out of wedlock
Knock on wooooood
I did contract some curable STDs
The embarrassment, guilt and fear
Haunted me
You would think that would make me
give up fornication for good
But my pleasure seeking did not cease
I'm human on the outside
On the inside... a beast
Searching for hot, black man flesh
On which to feast
I was the Energizer Bunny
Charged up and on beat
Menstrual cycle the only thing
that slowed me down
Besides yeast
Infections
I had goals
But being a hoe was not one of them
It's just the way things turned out
Everywhere, but in my own bed
Respond to that text message

Moremy Presents.... *The Celibacy Chronicles*

Hit 'em up girl, you already know
He gon' have weed and liquor galore
How u want it?
Let's explore
I had 'em on
Park benches
A plethora of car backseats
In house party bathroom closets
The beach
Having kinky adventures with
Men who weren't my Mister
Shied away from the church
Because I didn't want to face any ministers
Or my pastor
Who may have peeped my sinister path
I really wanted prayer
But didn't know how to ask...
After all this time
I sit back and laugh
The price of fun
Came at a big cost:
Broken mind, body, spirit
Confusion and love lost
It took feeling and being treated
Like a disposable semen receptacle
To finally realize my womb and I
are worthy of a respectable
Relationship
With oneself
This journey back to me
Would have to be a personal one
I needed my own help;
The advice from others left me stressed
Some days harder than others
But I'm doing my best

To stay in alignment
with the TRUE Spirit
Of my Self
I was created for more
Than being a closeted whore
When I started to love on me
My eyes opened up, I could finally see:
I don't have to chase a man to be noticed
I already beam
Bright
Like the light which was the first
thing spoken into creation
I now act out of self-love, no longer self-hatred
My self is sacred
And my stuff is gooooood
And now I've found love peace & wisdom
Just like I should....

Moremy Presents.... *The Celibacy Chronicles*

Artist: Ahanayzha Mabry

Spirits

When I'm drunk
a spirit takes over me.
Controlling me,
making me do things I don't wanna do
I do want to
but that I should just let be.

Sober, I'm a freak.
So when intoxicated
I feel even more elated
to let my inner freak be free.
Hormonal release.
How long have I known you?
or did we just meet?
Decisions, decisions
But I'm grown
so I know what's best for me...

My flesh speaks so loudly
Volumes as I walk across the room
All eyes on me.
Males and females tryna get a peek at my peach.
I'm intrigued
that you're that into me.
So now you're entering me
and as I can see pleasure and ecstasy
I also see you shouldn't have woken up next to me.
Someone tell me
how many drinks...
Did I have?
Did it take for me to be bad?
'Cause I never made love
I just pick and choose and fuck

Who doesn't love getting nuts?
I'm nuts
I'm wild, erotic
Freak was what they wanted
so freak was what I was
I got that line from Jill Scott
'Nothing Is For Nothing'
'cause sometimes after nuttin'
with a nobody whose body I borrowed
I feel like nothing
Numb to it all;
The pleasure, the pain
the fall
in character, will power and self-control.
I'm always putting celibacy on hold
so I can have one last go.
But who knows
when will be my last day here?
And my biggest fear, thing I'm enamored with the most
will be the one thing that'll take me outta here
I swear.
It's hard finding a balance between holding your liquor and lips.
Smooth talking, beautiful beings
and hips being navigated
like a captain of a ship
Sometimes I slip......

Moremy Presents.... *The Celibacy Chronicles*

Womb Rage

My womb is raging

Vulva pulsating

My body is telling me it's time for mating

But I'm waiting

Quite impatiently

Every attempt to fornicate

Falls under way

They busy

They have women

They have energies and drama that come along with them

That I don't desire to deal with

So I try to trick my mind and find other things to think about and do with my time

This is new for me

Ten years straight of sexual elation & now at twenty-six coming face to face with

Self-love and patience

Knowing thyself and hating that it took this long to find out

Has me feeling some kind of way

Suppressing daddy issues and conversations with my mother about my

experiences for fear I'll cause a trigger for her too

Orgasms were my frustrations taking their rightful place

Moremy Presents.... *The Celibacy Chronicles*

Often with the wrong people and motives

No questions ever asked by the guys about my sexual past

We all just learned to relax in the comfort of a warm space

Trust was risky

But we did it anyway

Searching for our high

Each other's drug of choice

Addicted to bad decisions

That felt so good

A rush

Going nowhere fast

So now I have to carry all the names of my immaturity to my future

Who was designed to cover and love me

This game isn't fair but it is reality

Daughters search for daddies in men destined to do her wrong

No man to model fathering skills in the home

To show her how Queens are treated and make her aware of her throne

So she single and out here trying to make love on her own

Wanting a bond that feels good and is long

Settling for less

Because no standards were in place

Just go with how you feel

Then life is created....

And now she has womb rage

Moremy Presents.... *The Celibacy Chronicles*

Mad that she's carrying a baby of a man who didn't know she was sacred and

relinquished his responsibility to have any place in their lives

Mad like so long ago she had dreams of a ring, but lost self-control

Mad like seats at tables discussing wedding invitations is null and void

Mad like elevator jams and traffic contractions

Baby don't deserve this type of life, *but my morals won't let me abort a blessing*

Funny cause morals were nowhere around when the texts were sent

Sex happened

Now you naked

Exposed

Extremely uncomfortable

Body calling you back home

This time for your own pain

Decisions made in the dark

Return to the light

Just makes her want to fight

The battle is internal

And will always be

Once we learn to tame that beast

Only then can we truly be free

Moremy Presents.... *The Celibacy Chronicles*

Artist: Ebonique Day aka Lady Picasso

Lust Demons

Got these lust demons pheining,
Screaming for a way to get on top
Don't take much
Wine, beer, henny and a lil' pop
That's when that freak come out
So nasty you can't stop
Any and everything coming
out ya mouth
I like all types of men
But I'm a sucka for the ones down south;
Southern drawl in my draws on best friend's couch
Anywhere here or there
Let's see how this plays out...

Hurt feelings, emotions
What's beyond this route?
Really need a release but
I'm feeling pressure not to hang out
Every time I do
We mix the gin and the juice
Somewhere laid out
Tryna prove a point to please his penis
All I need is love...
Church folks say *Call on Jesus*
But, I can't touch him physically
or feel him like I need 'em

This freedom...
To give of my body is so lethal
Substance abuse and narcotics
Make this easier to deal with

Let's heal this

But where do I begin?
Confess to myself (or someone else) my sins
Exuding patience to levitate greatness
Laying different places different faces
Progressing less is doing me in
It feels good for now
Until the pain starts to seep in
Next morning
Plan B's and "Wish It Wasn't Me's"
Crazy baby mama drama we never foresee
Tag team friend want in
Turn to have daughters and flee
This is you, this is me
This is us, this is we
This is no unpopular belief

Moremy Presents.... *The Celibacy Chronicles*

Artist: Sherrita C. Williams

Wake-Up Call

The saying goes

Three times the charm

But I've been attacked twice

And don't believe this is the smartest road to travel on

This road of risk

For the namesake of sexual bliss

Satisfied minutes of body contact

Cannot override the feeling of death

If I were to allow this disease to fester in me

My fallopian tubes and ovaries would become infected

Causing infertility in me

I need a cap of self-control

A steady partner

A condom in hand

An understanding that we ought to do this the safe way

I need the strength to not get weak

Learn to say "NO "without regret

I made the Dean's List

But wasn't smart enough to prevent this:

Moremy Presents.... *The Celibacy Chronicles*

Not smart enough to stop

Not smart enough to not even start

Not smart enough to wrap it up

Not smart enough to not mess with more than one person at a time

Not smart enough to just keep my legs shut

I could blame my stupidity

On an absent father, but why bother?

I could say this search of acceptance through sex

Stems from an encounter with childhood incest

But no,

I'll place the blame on me

Whose actions lead me to promiscuity

I'll take responsibility for the quick, thought-less actions

And lack of self-control

My reasons for self-hatred and sexual persuasion?

Hideous

Maybe that's why two times over

Chlamydia

Made her way into my bloodstream and pockets

Where money was used for medicine and doctor visitations

Callin' up more than one person 'cause I ain't know who had it

Moremy Presents.... *The Celibacy Chronicles*

Or who gave it to me

So I'll take responsibility

Stay to myself and learn to love her

I refuse to die at everyone else's expense

Just to be stimulated for a few minutes

Influenced

Growing up reading Zane + Cosmo magazines
Having Jada Fire, Pinky, and Cherokee D
as my favorite women on TV
Was not good
Hyper sexualized at an early age
Fornication was one of the only ways
I knew to connect
It didn't require much reflection

Impulse action was enough to gain satisfaction
Liquid libations always assisted lust to leak faster
Had to have it
Was never NOT an option
Just multiple choices
Of boys' numbers in my phone
Who would get a ring today?
Certainly not me
A future possibility wasn't motivation enough
to be sitting around waiting
On something not guaranteed
And to be honest, I don't know
if marriage is cut out for me
'Cause based on what I see;
All men desire more than one woman,
Will make a vow to you and still cheat
If not physically, emotionally or mentally
And in cases where fake love has put on a show so long
I'd rather remain free
Pick and choose who brings pleasure to me

Never seen my grandparents kiss
or sleep in the same bed

Meanwhile family tryna figure out
what's wrong with this girl?
While the homies brag on
how I'm infamous for head
I'm thinking I'm showing love
With the spread of my legs
Most asked once and didn't have to beg
My girlfriends switched from good
Girls to down for whateva
Let's make this a group thing
Save more covers
Exposing skin and sins
Proudly
That we could make eyes roll back and climax loudly

Sun rise, never discussing how
empty we all really felt inside
Just pull up your skirt and fasten your belts
Maybe breakfast in the mawnin'
To prove I'm a woman worthy of being around
But it never seems to work like that
I've spent more time beating myself up over the past
While I'm still carrying out the same actions
Could sex be my passion?
I spend the most time doing it
Screwing with my emotions...
When I can't even be open about how I feel
to the men getting all the feels
It's a thrill
Quite scary
Cause it's all voluntary
I learned to like it and be like this from somewhere...

Moremy Presents.... *The Celibacy Chronicles*

Artist: Nycci James

Moremy Presents.... *The Celibacy Chronicles*

Conservation with God

Lights (white) candles, some incense; sets out crystals that correlate with the 7 chakras. Sits in front of mirror with notepad, writing utensils and voice recorder on phone (prepared for when the ideas and affirmations arise.) Glass of water; a plant. Pours water into plant as I call out names of ancestors that have transitioned. Give thanks, ask for protection, wisdom and guidance from the powers that be that are in alignment with everything working out for my good.

Dear God,

Why am I still here? What is my purpose? I can't say I've done much intentional searching until now. Why was I misinformed early on? Why do I have to unlearn and relearn to know who I really am? Just so I can have a story to tell?

Dear God,

What does Chakras and Christ have to do with this really?

Everything is connected to you. So are the tangibles even necessary? There are poetry books with your words. You're one big author. We have imagination in common. I mostly talk to myself. Since I'm made in your image, when I write is it acting or lying? How is it that your spirit lives in me when I've done things and felt convicted after? It seems you allow disasters to occur quite frequently. Is this an example of blasphemy? Is masturbation really wrong? I mean, it's just me. How when even focusing on you, my body has natural tingling's?

Dear God,

Is this yoni egg going to really help me heal and love myself? I feel like I've fallen so deep. I know I need your help. Just haven't been myself. I remember the good little girl I used to be. I feel tainted and I wanna feel free. Why create a people if we always need help from each other? Really it's you we should reach to. They teach like you're in this outer realm; something in space and heaven, an external place. Not an internal exploration. You're involved in all unions. Love is ordained by you. Is there a soul mate for me, or will I always be a free spirit? Always "just friends", always just business...

I wanna be Jill Scott prepared. What if I don't ever get married? Am I supposed to find all my comfort in you? When can I ascend to my highest vibration? I think I'm over this lesson of patience. It's a daily struggle fighting temptation and too much libations. Why turn water into wine when grapes do the same thing? Why make men so fine and expect me to stay away? Why even give me eyes? Voluptuous breasts? Flesh.

Why is life a test that I'll either fail or pass? God forbid I come back. How can I hear you and not be confused if it's me? All the meditating in the world, yet thoughts always pop up in the most unnecessary times. How can I take control of my mind? I put my body on break so that I could hear you clearer. Cleansing the spirits of the many men I've encountered. I only want to elevate. To become the best version of me. I love you.

How can I improve?

MOREMY
Morgan Renae Myers

Instagram: @Moremy__

(double underscore)

Twitter: @Moremy__

(double underscore)

Facebook: @MorganRenaeMyers

Collaborative Artists

IN ORDER OF APPEARECNE

COVER ART: DARE COULTER
(ADARIA COULTER)
INSTAGRAM: DARECOULTER
FACEBOOK: DARECOULTER

1. **SEAN MULKEY**
   INSTAGRAM: SMULKEYARTS
   WEBSITE: WWW.ARTPAL.COM

2. **DAYLON OWENS**
   INSTAGRAM: DAYDAYTUPACART
   FACEBOOK: DAYLON OWENS

3. **TYAMICA MABRY**
   INSTAGRAM: TYPESOFHER
   FACEBOOK: TYPESOFHER
   EMAIL: TYPESOFHER@GMAIL.COM

4. **LYRICALUNIQSOUL**
   INSTAGRAM: LYRICALUNIQSOUL
   FACEBOOK: SYDNEY NICOLE A
   WEBSITE:
   WWW.SYDNEYNICOLECONSOL.WIXSITE.COM/WATERMELANINWANDERER
   EMAIL: SYDNEYNICOLECONSULTING@GMAIL.COM

5. **EBONIQUE DAY AKA LADY PICASSO**
   INSTAGRAM: EBONIQUE_AKA_LADY_PICASSO
   FACEBOOK: EBONIQUE DAY
   EMAIL: LASILKPRODUCTIONS@GMAIL.COM

6. **KALEYE**
   INSTAGRAM: KALEYE_
   FACEBOOK: KALEYE_
   WWW.KALEYEBEAUTYMAGIC.COM
   DDESJONNE@YAHOO.COM

7. **KENDRA WASHINGTON**
   INSTAGRAM: KENDRAWASHINGTON_
   FACEBOOK: KENDRA WASHINGTON
   WEBSITE: WWW.KENDRAWASHINGTON.COM
   EMAIL: KENDRAWASHINGTON30@GMAIL.COM

8. **DR. HOW**
   INSTAGRAM: DR__HOW
   FACEBOOK: FACEBOOK.COM/DHOWELL723
   EMAIL: DHOWELL7233@GMAIL.COM

9. **ERRAN HAMLIN**
   INSTAGRAM: ERRANZART
   FACEBOOK: ERRANZART

10. **AHANAYZHA MABRY**
    INSTAGRAM: A_NAYZH
    FACEBOOK: AHANAYZHA MABRY

11. SHERRITA C. WILLIAMS
    INSTAGRAM: SHEWILL247
    FACEBOOK: SHERRITA C. WILLIAMS
    EMAIL: ESOENTNC@GMAIL.COM

12. NYCCI JAMES
    INSTAGRAM: ARTNSOUL360
    FACEBOOK: FB.ME/ARTNSOUL36

www.ingramcontent.com/pod-product-compliance
Lightning Source LLC
Chambersburg PA
CBHW042341150426
43196CB00001B/16